W9-ABL-697

Bug Jokes

What do bees wear to school?

Yellow jackets.

COMPILED BY PAM ROSENBERG • ILLUSTRATED BY BOB OSTROM

The Child's World®

Special thanks to Katie Cottrell for her
assistance in compiling source materials.

Published by The Child's World®
1980 Lookout Drive • Mankato, MN 56003-1705
800-599-READ • www.childsworld.com

Acknowledgments
The Child's World®: Mary Berendes, Publishing Director
The Design Lab: Design
Jody Jensen Shaffer: Editing

ISBN 9781623239947
LCCN 2013947269

Printed in the United States of America
Mankato, MN
November, 2013
PA02196

ANTS

What game do ants play with elephants? Squash.

What do ants take when they are sick? Ant-ibiotics.

What kind of ant can break a picnic table with one hit? A gi-ant.

What's the biggest ant in the world? An eleph-ant.

Why was the baby ant so confused? Because all of its uncles were ants.

What's smaller than an ant's dinner? An ant's mouth.

Why do bees hum?
Because they don't know the words.

What do bees chew?
Bumblegum

How do bees comb their hair?
With a honeycomb.

What is a bee's favorite song?
"Stingin' in the Rain"

What kind of animal says zzub?
A bee flying backwards.

What goes "hum-choo, hum-choo"?
A bee with a cold.

What do you call a young bee?
A babe-bee.

What kind of weapon goes "buzz, buzz" when you pull the trigger?
A bee-bee gun.

Where does a bee sit?
On his bee-hind.

What does a bee order at McDonald's?
A humburger.

What did the bee say to the flower?
Hey, Bud, when do you open?

What did the bee say to the flower?
Hello, Honey!

What did one bee say to the other bee during the summer?
Swarm in here, isn't it?

BUTTERFLIES AND MOTHS

What's the biggest moth in the world?
The mammoth.

What's green and dangerous?
A caterpillar with a bad temper.

What do insects learn at school?
Mothmatics.

Why did the caterpillar go to the library?
He wanted to be a bookworm.

ANNA: Why is there a moth in my soup?
SCHOOL COOK: The fly must be on vacation!

What do you get when you eat caterpillars? Butterflies in your stomach.

Why couldn't the butterfly go to the dance? Because it was a moth ball.

Why was the little insect crying?

It wanted its moth-er.

12

FLEAS

What kind of celebrations do fleas in Mexico have?
Flea-estas.

What's the difference between a flea and a wolf?
One prowls on the hairy and the other howls on the prairie.

What do you get if you cross a rabbit and a flea?
Bugs Bunny.

What's the best place to buy bugs?
At a flea market.

Who can leap tall poodles in a single bound?
Super Flea!

How do fleas travel?
They itch-hike.

13

FLIES

DINER: Waiter, there's a fly in my soup!
WAITER: Well, keep quiet about it, or everyone will want one.

How do you keep flies out of the kitchen?
Put a pile of manure in the living room.

What's the difference between a fly and a bird?
A bird can fly, but a fly can't bird!

CUSTOMER: What is this fly doing in my soup?
WAITER: I think he's doing the backstroke.

What has four wheels and flies?
A garbage truck.

What do you call a fly without wings?
A walk.

What has four legs and flies?
A picnic table.

Why did the flies go to Paris?
Because they wanted to be French flies.

If there are five flies in the kitchen, how do you know which one is a football player?
He's the one in the sugar bowl.

GRASSHOPPERS AND CRICKETS

What's an insect's favorite game?

What do you call a bug that jumps over cups?
A glasshopper.

What's green and can jump a mile in a minute?
A grasshopper with hiccups.

Cricket.

MOSQUITOES

What's a mosquito's favorite sport?
Skin diving.

What do you get if you cross the Lone Ranger with a mosquito?
The Masked-quito!

What did the mosquito say the first time it saw a camel?
Did I do that?

When are mosquitoes most annoying?
When they get under your skin.

What has six legs and talks in code?
A Morse-quito.

What do you get when you cross a mosquito with a hippo?
I'm not sure, but if it stings you, you'll be in big trouble!

MISCELLANEOUS BUG JOKES

What kind of bugs live in clocks?
Ticks.

What do you get if you cross the Beatles with the Rolling Stones?
The Squashed Bugs.

How do fireflies start a race?
"Ready, set, glow!"

Why did the insect get kicked out of the park?
He was a litterbug.

What do you call a bug with four wheels and a trunk?
A Volkswagen Beetle.
In the opening words, "In the Big Inning."

Where do they take sick insects?
To the wasp-ital.

What does a baby bug ride in?
A buggy.

SARAH: Mommy, are bugs good to eat?

MOM: Let's not talk about bugs at dinner.

MOM (AFTER DINNER):
Now what did you want to ask me?

SARAH: Oh, never mind. There was a bug in my stew, but now it's gone!

PATIENT: Doctor, what is the best way to prevent diseases caused by biting insects?

DOCTOR: Don't bite any!

What do you get if you cross a bee with a skunk?
An animal that stinks and stings.

What is a centipede's favorite toy?
Leg-os.

What is a tick's favorite game?
Tic-tac-toe.

What do insects use to write reports?
Flypaper.

Why was the centipede late for school?
    Because he was playing "This Little Piggy" with his baby brother.

What do you get if you cross a centipede with a chicken?
    Enough drumsticks to feed an army.

How do we know that insects are smart?
    They always know when we're eating outside.

What's worse than an alligator with a toothache?
    A centipede with athlete's foot.

A farmer was milking his cow when a bug flew into the barn. The bug circled the farmer's head, then flew into the cow's ear. The farmer didn't think much about it until the bug squirted out into his bucket. It had gone in one ear and out the udder.

About Bob Ostrom:

Bob Ostrom has been illustrating children's books for nearly twenty years. A graduate of the New England School of Art & Design at Suffolk University, Bob has worked for such companies as Disney, Nickelodeon, and Cartoon Network. He lives in North Carolina with his wife, Melissa, and three children, Will, Charlie, and Mae.

About Pam Rosenberg:

Pam Rosenberg is a former junior high school teacher and corporate trainer. She currently works as a author, editor, and the mother of Sarah and Jake. She took on this project as a service to all her fellow parents of young children. At least now their kids will have lots of jokes to choose from when looking for the one they will tell their parents over and over and over again!